我的第一本中文故事书·小美的故事系
MY FIRST CHINESE STORYBOOKS · THE STORIES OF XIAO

策划：英国谢菲尔德大学孔子学院
编委：赵　霞　王　慧　罗素芳

Pumpkin Lanterns

Compiled by Chen Shan（陈珊　编著）
Illustrated by Jiu Ye（九野　插画）

First Edition 2021

ISBN 978-7-5138-2039-4

Published by Sinolingua Co., Ltd
24 Baiwanzhuang Street, Beijing 100037, China
Tel: (86) 10-68320585 68997826
Fax: (86) 10-68997826 68326333
http://www.sinolingua.com.cn
E-mail: hyjx@sinolingua.com.cn
Facebook: www.facebook.com/sinolingua
Printed by Beijing Xicheng Printing Co., Ltd

Printed in the People's Republic of China

How to use this book

Students can use this book with the help of a parent or teacher to practise their listening, speaking, reading, and writing skills through the following exercises, which should be selected according to the ability of the students.

1. Following the examples in Appendix 1, select about ten key-words for intensive pronunciation practice. This will help the students read the whole story smoothly. The students can glance over other new words to better understand the story.

2. Read through the book and comprehend the story. Repeated phrases and sentences will eventually help the students to read the book fluently without referring to pinyin.

3. Listen to words or sentences from the book and find their matching pictures.

4. Select a few commonly used words. Practise writing and memorising them.

5. Practise the key sentences that are frequently used in the book.

6. Cover the words and pinyin. Retell the story using only the pictures in the book with the help of your teacher or parents.

7. Use the words you have learnt to substitute the words in the key sentence structures and then practise those sentences as well. This will help you learn by association and review the knowledge.

8. For a review, do the exercises in Appendix 2.

9. After reading the story, answer the questions in Appendix 3.

10. Parents and teachers can prepare activities to let the students experience the fun of nature. See Appendix 4.

用书说明（供参考）

在用此书学习中文时，学生可在老师或家长的帮助下通过以下项目进行听说读写的全面练习。可根据学生中文程度的不同，选择合适的练习项目。

1. 生词学习（说）：参考附录一选出 10 个左右在本册出现的重要生词进行发音练习，为下一步阅读全文打下基础。其他生词可一带而过，只是帮助理解故事。
2. 阅读练习（读）：边读句子边理解故事，利用重复的词和句逐步摆脱拼音，最后能流利地读出全文。
3. 听力练习（听）：听生词发音，找出其对应的图画；再听句子，找出该句子对应的插图。
4. 书写练习（写）：选一些最常用的生词练习笔画，边写边记。
5. 句型练习（听、说、语法）：针对本册反复出现的核心句型进行操练。
6. 看图说话（说）：盖住拼音和汉字，在老师或家长的帮助下看图说出故事。
7. 句型替换练习（复习巩固）：用以前学过的词汇套用本册核心句型再进行操练，可举一反三和复习。
8. 词汇理解练习：见附录二，复习所学的词汇。
9. 针对故事回答问题（阅读理解）：见附录三。
10. 活动参与（玩）：家长或老师可组织活动，带学生体验亲近自然的乐趣，见附录四。

Pumpkins become ripe during Halloween season. An annual plant, its vine can grow several metres, and the yellow flowers look just like trumpets. Pumpkins can not only be made into lamps when Halloween comes, but they are also delicious food. Rich in nutrition, they are the ingredient for many kinds of dishes and desserts.

October 31 is Halloween. Mum bought a pumpkin and brought it home.

Shí yuè sānshíyī hào shì Wànshèngjié , māma mǎile yí gè dà nánguā
10月31号是万圣节，妈妈买了一个大南瓜

huíjiā .
回家。

Xiaomei helped Mum to empty the seeds. They were going to make a Halloween jack-o'-lantern.

Māma gēn Xiǎoměi yìqǐ bǎ nánguāzǐ dōu tāo chūlai, yào zuò yí
妈妈跟小美一起把南瓜籽都掏出来，要做一

gè Wànshèngjié nánguādēng.
个万圣节南瓜灯。

Mum wanted to make a ghost face on the pumpkin, but Xiaomei wanted to make a kitty face.

Māma yào zuò yí gè guǐ liǎn, Xiǎoměi yào zuò yí gè xiǎo māo liǎn.
妈妈要做一个鬼脸，小美要做一个小猫脸。

Dad said they could make two faces on one pumpkin — a ghost face on the front and a kitty face on the back.

Bàba shuō nà jiù zài yí gè nánguā shang zuò liǎng gè liǎn . Qiánmiàn shì
爸爸说那就在一个南瓜上做两个脸。前面是
guǐ liǎn , hòumiàn shì xiǎo māo liǎn .
鬼脸，后面是小猫脸。

The jack-o'-lantern was finished. They put a candle inside the lantern, lit it, and put the pumpkin lantern on the doorstep.

Nánguādēng zuòhǎo le. Tāmen zài lǐmiàn diǎnshàng làzhú, fàng zài mén
南瓜灯做好了。他们在里面点上蜡烛，放在门

qián de táijiē shang.
前的台阶上。

Kids from all the nearby streets came to see the pumpkin lantern.

Jǐ tiáo jiē de xiǎopéngyǒu dōu lái Xiǎoměi jiā mén qián kàn nánguādēng .
几条街的小朋友都来小美家门前看南瓜灯。

Some of them wanted to see the ghost face, and some of them wanted to see the kitty face, so everyone scrambled to see the one they liked. Bang—! The jack-o'-lantern fell over and broke.

Yǒu rén yào kàn qiánmiàn de guǐ liǎn, yǒu rén yào kàn hòumiàn de xiǎo māo
有人要看前面的鬼脸，有人要看后面的小猫

liǎn, dàjiā dōu yào zhēngzhe kàn. Pā! Nánguādēng shuāipò le.
脸，大家都要争着看。啪！南瓜灯摔破了。

Xiaomei was so sad and wept.

Xiǎoměi shāngxīn de kū le .
小美伤心地哭了。

Mum said, “Don’t worry! We have the pumpkin seeds. We can plant them next year. We will have many pumpkins to make lanterns with all different faces then.”

Māma shuō: "Bú yàojǐn, wǒmen hái yǒu nánguāzǐ. Míngnián chūntiān
妈妈说："不要紧，我们还有南瓜籽。明年春天
wǒmen zhòng hěn duō nánguā, kěyǐ zuò hěn duō bùtóng yàngzi de
我们种很多南瓜，可以做很多不同样子的
nánguādēng."
南瓜灯。"

Next year when spring came, Xiaomei planted the pumpkin seeds in her backyard.

Chūntiān lái le , Xiǎoměi bǎ nánguāzǐ zhòng dào hòuyuàn .

春天来了，小美把南瓜籽种到后院。

It was sunny during the day and rainy at night. The new green pumpkin shoots soon came out.

Báitiān shàizhe tàiyáng, wǎnshang xiàzhe xiǎoyǔ, lǜlǜ de nánguā miáo zhǎng chūlai la.

白天晒着太阳，晚上下着小雨，绿绿的南瓜苗长出来啦。

In summer, the pumpkin plants started flowering, and a lot of green pumpkins appeared.

Xiàtiān, nánguā kāichū huánghuáng de huā, jiéchū hǎoduō hǎoduō xiǎo nánguā.

夏天，南瓜开出黄黄的花，结出好多好多小南瓜。

In autumn, the pumpkins were golden.

Qiūtiān lái le, nánguā biàn de jīnhuáng jīnhuáng de.
秋天来了，南瓜变得金黄金黄的。

Xiaomei and her mum gave some pumpkins to their neighbours.

Xiǎoměi hé māma bǎ nánguā sòng gěi línjūmen .
小美和妈妈把南瓜送给邻居们。

That year when Halloween came, jack-o'-lanterns appeared at every family's doorstep, and each had a different face.

Zhè yì nián de Wànshèngjié , měi jiā mén qián dōu fàngle nánguādēng ,
这一年的万圣节，每家门前都放了南瓜灯，

měi ge nánguādēng dōu yǒu bù yíyàng de liǎn .
每个南瓜灯都有不一样的脸。

Appendix 1

New words:

万圣节 Wànshèngjié (Halloween)

南瓜 nánguā (pumpkin)

籽 zǐ (seed)

掏出 tāochū (pull out)

鬼脸 guǐ liǎn (grimace)

摔破 shuāipò (to break)

邻居 línjū (neighbour)

脸 liǎn (face)

Appendix 2

Fill in the blanks.

1. 万圣节是在每年的 _____ 月 ______ 号。
2. 南瓜是一种 ________________。
3. 南瓜花是 ________ 颜色的。
4. 南瓜应该在 _______ 播种。

True(√) or false(×).

1. 小美妈妈买回家两个南瓜。 (　　)

2. 小美做了一个南瓜灯。 ( )

3. 小美的南瓜灯被打碎了。 ( )

4. 小美把南瓜送给了同学。 ( )

Fill in the blanks with the given characters.

A. 来 B. 掏 C. 把 D. 点

1. 妈妈跟小美一起把南瓜籽都 ____ 出来。
2. 南瓜灯做好了，里面 ____ 上蜡烛。
3. 几条街的小朋友都 _____ 小美家门前看南瓜灯。
4. 春天来了，小美 _____ 南瓜籽种到后院。

Form sentences according to the story.

例：一个 爸爸说 两个脸 南瓜上 那就 做 。

爸爸说那就一个南瓜上做两个脸。

1. 大南瓜 妈妈 一个 回家 买了 。

____

2. 后院　小美　种到　南瓜籽　把

____

3. 开出　夏天　黄黄的花　南瓜　。

____

4. 送给　小美　把　妈妈　邻居们　和　南瓜　。

____

Appendix 3

Answer the questions.

1. Do you like Halloween? There is a Chinese festival that is similar to Halloween. What is it?
2. What kind of jack-o'-lantern do you like best?
3. Do you know how a pumpkin grows?

Appendix 4

Try to finish the tasks.

1. Share your story of an unforgettable Halloween.
2. Make a jack-o'-lantern with your teacher and classmates.

出版策划：王君校　韩　晖
统筹协调：付　眉　韩　颖　彭　博
责任编辑：翟淑蓉
英文编辑：薛彧威
封面设计：九　野
责任印制：汪　洋

图书在版编目（CIP）数据

我的第一本中文故事书．小美的故事系列．4，南瓜灯：汉英对照／陈珊编著．-- 北京：华语教学出版社，2021.3
ISBN 978-7-5138-2039-4

Ⅰ．①我… Ⅱ．①陈…Ⅲ．①汉语－对外汉语教学－教学参考资料 Ⅳ．① H195.4

中国版本图书馆 CIP 数据核字（2020）第 221808 号

南瓜灯

陈珊　编著　九野 插画

*

华语教学出版社有限责任公司出版
（中国北京百万庄大街 24 号　邮政编码 100037）
电话：(86)10-68320585　68997826
传真：(86)10-68997826　68326333
网址：www.sinolingua.com.cn
电子信箱：hyjx@sinolingua.com.cn
北京玺诚印务有限公司印刷
2021 年（16 开）第 1 版
2021 年第 1 版第 1 次印刷
（汉英）
ISBN 978-7-5138-2039-4
002500